THE VICTORIANS

CONTENTS

COUNTRY LIFE

While new technology and machinery improved the efficiency and profitability of many farms, for most people the industrial revolution of the 18th and 19th centuries was a period of massive upheaval and social change. Many people lost their jobs and their homes, since most houses were tied to their occupations and they were forced to seek work elsewhere.

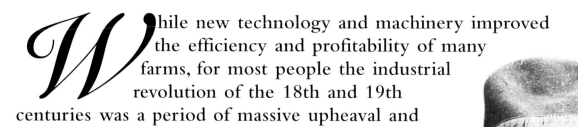

NEW MACHINERY

New machinery, such as this steam traction engine, was very versatile and could do the work of several men. In the space of a few years the heavy horses, that formerly pulled ploughs and other agricultural machinery, became obsolete.

ANIMAL HUSBANDRY

While those involved in agriculture suffered enormously at the hands of 'progress', many of those who tended animals, such as cattle herders and shepherds, were little affected by the technological revolution sweeping the land; survivors from a pre-industrial age.

COUNTRY AIR

Although many of those who worked in the country still lived in primitive, one-roomed cottages, living conditions and sanitation were much better than in town slums.

CHANGING MARKETPLACE

Many villages lost their weekly market as more and more of the food produced was taken to the towns to feed their burgeoning populations. A single village shop, selling a range of goods, could usually satisfy the needs of most rural communities.

LIFE EXPECTANCY

Although generally less well-off than town dwellers, those who lived in the country usually had a better quality of life and could expect to live longer; about 50 years of age compared to 40 for those in towns.

OUR DAILY BREAD

In 1815 Corn Laws had been passed to keep grain prices high and protect England from cheap imports, but these were repealed in 1846 to facilitate free trade. The result was a fall in the price of bread, though farmers were affected badly as a consequence.

LIFE IN TOWNS

*A*t the beginning of Victoria's reign (1837) only about 20% of the population lived in towns, but by 1901, when she died, this figure had risen to about 75%. During this period the population of Britain doubled from around 20 million to 40 million. Most people moved to towns to find work in the factories, Rows of poor quality terraced slums sprang up around the factories to house them.

VICTIMS OF CIRCUMSTANCE

Poverty was so bad in most towns that many people resorted to crime in the dingy streets. The old and infirm, particularly, often fell victim to pickpockets.

POOR SANITATION

Sanitary conditions in Victorian towns were often very poor. Only the rich could afford proper toilet facilities. The poor had to share a communal lavatory, usually just a shed over a hole in the ground treated with quicklime to dissolve effluent. Few houses had running water or drains and it was a daily task to empty slops down open gullies in the streets.

HOMELESSNESS

Homelessness was a constant problem in towns, especially for those who were unable to work, who were literally put out onto the streets. Alcohol was cheap (beer was less than 1p per pint) and easier to acquire than good drinking water, so drunkenness was a problem, even amongst children.

STREET TRADERS

The streets offered numerous opportunities to earn a living. Traders sold their wares, such as bread, milk and pies, from hand carts. Girls might sell cut flowers while boys might offer fresh poultry or a shoeshine.

COMPARATIVE LIFESTYLES

These two views show the comparison between the poor and wealthy sectors of 19th century towns. The rich could afford elegant, well-built villas, while the poor had to tolerate the squalor of cramped, back-to-back housing surrounded by noise and filth.

LIFE FOR THE RICH

THE HIGH LIFE

For many wealthy young ladies life was an endless round of social gatherings, attending balls, the opera or the theatre, so as to be seen by prospective husbands.

The Victorian age saw the emergence of a new tier of social class, wealthy businessmen who made vast fortunes from the new advances in technology, though often at the expense of the working classes who were forced to work in appalling conditions for low wages. Until the rise of the Victorian industrial entrepreneurs, most of the country's wealth lay in land ownership, particularly the estates of the aristocracy, but now any enterprising individual could become rich.

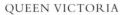
A STITCH IN TIME

New technology and mass-production brought many labour-saving devices, including the sewing machine. This sewing machine, manufactured by Wheeler and Wilson, is considered to be the forerunner of the modern lock-stitch and revolutionised clothes manufacture.

QUEEN VICTORIA

- *Born 1819*
- *Ascended the throne 1837*
- *Died 1901*

Victoria was proud of the technical achievements of her reign and allowed many new devices to be used in the royal household, such as electric lighting and carpet cleaners.

CHARITY STATUS

A charity matinee´ for a light comedy performance at the Theatre Royal, in London's Haymarket. Theatre-going in general was very fashionable, but it soon became popular, and almost essential for social advancement, to be seen at charitable events.

FINE TABLEWARE

Fine porcelain and bone china tableware became extremely fashionable among the aristocracy and rising middle-classes. Improved methods of manufacture meant that items could be mass-produced, but retained their 'hand-made' quality.

THE SPOKEN WORD

The phonograph, the forerunner of today's hi-fi, was invented by Thomas Edison in 1877. Apart from the recording of music one of the earliest uses suggested by Edison was talking books for the blind.

THE POOR AT HOME

Although the technological revolution brought wealth to industrialists, it brought abject poverty to the working classes. Many were forced to work long hours, under appalling conditions, for low wages. Many chose to emigrate to Australia, America and Canada. One way out of the poverty trap was to work in service in the houses of the wealthy. There were over one million domestic servants in 1851 out of a population of just 20 million.

DESTITUTION

Many of the homeless lived in workhouses where, in payment for working during the day, they received a meal and a bed. This old woman was so destitute that she could not work and slept on the steps of the workhouse. She minded a friend's baby in return for food.

CHILDREN'S HOMES

Homelessness was an ever-growing problem in towns, particularly among children, whose parents might have died. Dr. Thomas Barnado opened his first home for poor boys (many of whom had run away to escape the cruelty of factory conditions) in London in 1870, providing them with food and shelter.

PAWNBROKERS

In an age before pensions and welfare benefits, if a poor family fell upon hard times they were forced to sell or pawn their possessions to support themselves. This was especially true for widows whose incomes ceased when their husband died.

LEARNING BY ROTE

Few working class children received any education because it was felt it would make them discontent with their lot. The fortunate few went to dame schools, charitable institutions run by women in their own homes, where reading, writing and simple arithmetic were taught.

COTTAGE INDUSTRIES

It was not uncommon for poor couples to have as many as 9 or 10 children. Although this view shows a typical family with the children at play (probably on a Sunday, the only day of rest) the whole family was expected to work. Even those children not sent out to work in factories and mills had to help support the family by doing chores around the house or making items for sale.

FOOD & DRINK

One of the biggest problems facing Victorian society was how to feed a population that was growing at an alarming rate. In pre-industrial Britain, the majority of people worked on the land and produced their own food. Most people now worked in factories and had to buy all their food with their wages, marking the beginnings of the modern consumer society.

DELIVERED TO YOUR DOOR

Milk was delivered straight from the farm. Customers took their jugs out into the street to the milkman, who filled them from large churns.

SPOILT FOR CHOICE

Never before had such a range of foods been available as cheap imports flooded in from abroad. Even the meagre diets of the poor gradually improved and became more varied. Such items as tea, for long an expensive luxury, became affordable by all.

CONVENIENCE FOODS

One of the solutions to keeping food fresh was this dry-air syphon refrigerator (c.1900). Food was chilled by the insulation of ice blocks in an adjoining compartment, which circulated cold air. Towards the end of the Victorian era tinned foods also became available.

HOME DELIVERIES

In smaller towns, and in villages, street tradesmen still carried their wares from door-to-door. Fresh bread, fish, dairy products and vegetables were often sold this way, but in larger towns, especially towards the end of the 19th century, improved standards of hygiene meant that more and more people bought their food from shops, where it was better protected.

THE MIDDLE MAN

Markets are a survival from the pre-industrialised age, when few shops existed and buyers and sellers met to exchange goods. At town wholesale markets, like Covent Garden fruit and vegetable market in London, shown here, larger traders bought goods in bulk from several suppliers at cheaper prices, which they then sold on to smaller traders for a profit.

PASTIMES

A GAME FOR GENTLEMEN

Cricket, first played in the 16th century, grew in popularity and became a gentleman's pursuit. W.G. Grace, perhaps the most famous cricketer of all time, lifted the game to its present status. He had an active playing career of 35 years and on one occasion amassed the score of 224 not out.

For most people Sunday was the only day when they did not have to work, so many simply rested. For others, cheap railway transport meant that for the first time they could visit other areas. Day trips to seaside towns became popular, as did visits to the growing number of public art galleries and museums.

CHILDREN'S ENTERTAINMENT

Children in rural areas were sometimes treated to a performance by a travelling puppeteer with his 'Punch and Judy' show, a survival from medieval fairs.

THE NOUVEAU RICH

The wealth generated by industry created a new breed of entrepreneurs who amassed large, disposable incomes. Gambling had always been popular, but exclusive casinos and gentlemen's clubs were established in an attempt to legitimise the pursuit.

I SAY, I SAY, I SAY ....

Every town could boast at least one, in many cases several, theatres and music halls, showing everything from variety shows to plays, opera and ballet. In the 1890s over 350 music halls opened in London alone.

THE DAY OF SETTLEMENT

These characters are settling their debts at the Derby. Gambling on sporting events has always been popular, but never more so than in Victorian times. It was one of the rare occasions when people from different backgrounds mixed socially.

TRADITIONAL SKILLS

Traditional needlework and embroidery skills remained the main pastime for many middle and upper class ladies. This design has been used for the title page of a children's book on dolls' houses, the manufacture of which became extremely popular in Victorian times.

BESIDE THE SEASIDE

Although the benefits of sea bathing had been discovered in the 18th century, it was the coming of the railway age that made seaside excursions possible for the masses.

FASHION

A FULLER FIGURE

By about 1870 bustles replaced crinoline. Skirts were draped over a frame of padded cushions to give more fullness to the back of the dress.

As is the case in all ages, clear distinctions were drawn between the fashions worn by people from different social backgrounds. The poor invariably wore clothes that were practical, giving few concessions to fashion, while the rich could afford better materials and indulge themselves in more elaborate styles, purely for the look, even though many were extremely uncomfortable to wear. People from all classes tended to keep a special set of clothes for Sunday best.

FASHION CONSCIOUSNESS

Narrow waists were very fashionable for ladies, right up to the end of Victoria's reign. This was achieved by wearing corsets made of steel, wood or bone, which were so tightly laced that they restricted breathing, causing some women to faint.

FASHION ACCESSORIES

Ladies carried many fashion accessories, particularly when attending social functions. In addition to jewellery, they might carry a fan, such as the one shown here, complete with artificial flower decoration. Hair styles were more elaborate, often incorporating wigs and false hair pieces. Gentlemen usually carried gloves and a walking cane.

CHANGING FACE OF FASHION

The invention of the sewing machine did not make seamstresses, tailors and shoemakers redundant (in 1891 over a quarter of a million people worked in clothes manufacture) but instead made more elaborate designs possible. Ladies' shoes in particular became far more daring in their design as a result of mechanisation. Gentlemen wore spats, short cloth gaiters below their trouser bottoms to protect their shoes from mud.

FOLLOWERS OF FASHION

Working class children wore cast-offs or cut-down adult clothes, while wealthier families dressed their children very formally in miniature versions of adult styles. Boys and girls both wore dresses until about five years old.

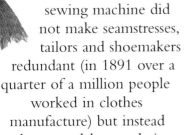

COSTUME JEWELLERY

Many precious and semi-precious stones were imported from the east, particularly from India, where they were quite common, and used to decorate items of fashion jewellery.

ART &
ARCHITECTURE

*V*ictorian art and architecture was often dismissed as contributing nothing new and original. While they did produce the Gothic and Classical revivals, the development of graceful structures, such as bridges and canopies using iron, steel and glass are wholly their own. Literary giants like Charles Dickens, Sir Walter Scott and the Brontë sisters developed the novel to its full potential, while probably the most original group of English painters, the Pre-Raphaelites, emerged during this time when Millais, Rossetti, Hunt and other like-minded artists formed a school of art that reflected the spirit of the age.

SPOKESMAN FOR THE AGE

Charles Dickens (1812-70) was the greatest and most popular novelist of his day. His graphic descriptions of Victorian England give us a good idea of what life was really like, particularly for the poor. All of his books were serialised, making them available to all classes.

THE CRYSTAL PALACE

The Great Exhibition of 1851 was the brainchild of Prince Albert and was housed in the purpose-built Crystal Palace. It was a masterpiece of cast iron and glass, designed by Joseph Paxton, covering 26 acres and measuring three times the length of St. Paul's Cathedral. Incredibly the building survived a move from Hyde Park to Sydenham after the exhibition, but sadly burned down in 1936.

Many art galleries and museums opened in towns throughout Britain to educate the masses and introduce ordinary people to the wider world of art.

TRAGIC GENIUS

The Brontë sisters, Anne, Emily and Charlotte, all wrote under male pseudonyms to improve their chances of success. They lived in lonely isolation on the Yorkshire moors and died within seven years of one another, all at young ages.

BOB CRATCHIT & TINY TIM

Bob Cratchit and Tiny Tim are two famous characters from Dickens's first, and best-known, 'Christmas book', *A Christmas Carol*. In this novel, the simple enjoyment of the poor Cratchit family is contrasted with the tight-fisted attitude of the miser, Ebenezer Scrooge. Dressed in threadbare clothes, with his crippled son to look after, the fate of Bob Cratchitt and his family is instrumental in Scrooge's eventual discovery of the true meaning of Christmas.

TONY WELLER

The appearance of Tony Weller in The Pickwick Papers ensured the success of the book. Samuel Pickwick meets Tony Weller at the White Hart Inn, Borough.

He is described as wearing *'a coarse-striped waistcoat, with black calico sleeves and blue glass buttons; drab breeches and leggings. A bright red handkerchief was wound in a very loose and unstudied style round his neck.'*

LITTLE NELL

Nell Trent is the central figure in *The Old Curiosity Shop*. Her character is drawn partly from Dickens's sister-in-law, Mary (see page 11), who died suddenly in the author's arms not long after his marriage to Catherine. Dickens poured all his feelings into the fictional death of Little Nell, writing to the illustrator of the book *'I am breaking my heart over this story.'*

THE WORK OF CHARLES DICKENS

Dickens portrays all of Victorian society in his novels, from the aristocracy to the poorest of the working classes, and he was a keen observer of humanity. His books are full of larger-than-life characters, but Dickens was also fascinated by ordinary, middle-class people and their often rather shabby, mundane lives. In one of the Sketches by Boz, he wrote: 'It is strange with how little notice, good, bad or indifferent, a man may live and die in London. His existence is a matter of interest to no one save himself; he cannot be said to be forgotten when he dies, for no one remembered him when he was alive.'

GHOSTLY PAINTING

This painting by Robert William Buss is titled Dickens's Dream. It shows Dickens surrounded by the ghostly outlines of characters and scenes from his books. After Dickens's death, G.H. Lewes, the partner of George Eliot, wrote: *'the joys and pains of childhood, the petty tyrannies of ignoble natures, the genial pleasantries of happy natures, the life of the poor, the struggles of the street and back parlour, the insolence of office… these he could deal with so we laughed and cried'.*

BETSY TROTWOOD

David Copperfield's great-aunt, Betsy Trotwood, is one of the most endearing of all Dickens's characters. She has a sharp tongue and a heart of gold, and wages a daily battle against the donkeys that invade the lawn in front of her house. David notes *'To this hour I don't know whether my aunt had any lawful right of way over that patch of green; but she had settled it in her own mind that she had. The one great outrage of her life… was the passage of a donkey over that immaculate spot.'*

HEALTH & MEDICINE

The main health problem facing Victorians, particularly in the towns, was that of overcrowding and the public health problems associated with it. The large numbers of people living in the densely packed slum houses produced a lot of waste, but there was no proper means to dispose of it. Streets became open sewers which led to many outbreaks of diseases such as typhoid and cholera. A series of Public Health Acts from 1848 on were passed in Parliament making it the responsibility of local councils to provide drainage and clean water supplies and clear away slums.

THE WATER CLOSET

As sewerage systems improved so flushable toilets became more common in rich households. The poor usually shared a communal 'earth closet' outside, which was often relocated as the cesspit beneath it filled with effluent.

MEDIEVAL CURES

Prior to the discovery in around 1856 by such scientists as Louis Pasteur that disease was caused by microscopic bacteria, medical knowledge had advanced little since the middle ages. Crude treatments, like blood-letting to remove toxins, were still widely practiced.

SHOCK TACTICS

In 1867 Joseph Lister developed an antiseptic to kill bacteria, which increased the survival rate from surgery dramatically. Prior to that over half of patients died from shock, gangrene or secondary infections.

POOR DIET

Many children, deprived of sunlight and clean air, and fed a poor, unbalanced diet, developed rickets, a debilitating disease causing bone malformation. Fresh milk containing plenty of vitamin D helped reduce the incidence of the disease.

WATERBORNE DISEASES

Following numerous outbreaks of typhoid and cholera in overcrowded towns, a link was discovered by Edwin Chadwick between disease and poor living conditions. Massive sewers were constructed to improve the drainage and carry dirty water out to sea.

DENTAL HYGIENE

This Victorian dentist's surgery shows treadle-operated drills. The successful use of chloroform as an anaesthetic after 1847 made it possible to remove teeth or perform operations painlessly.

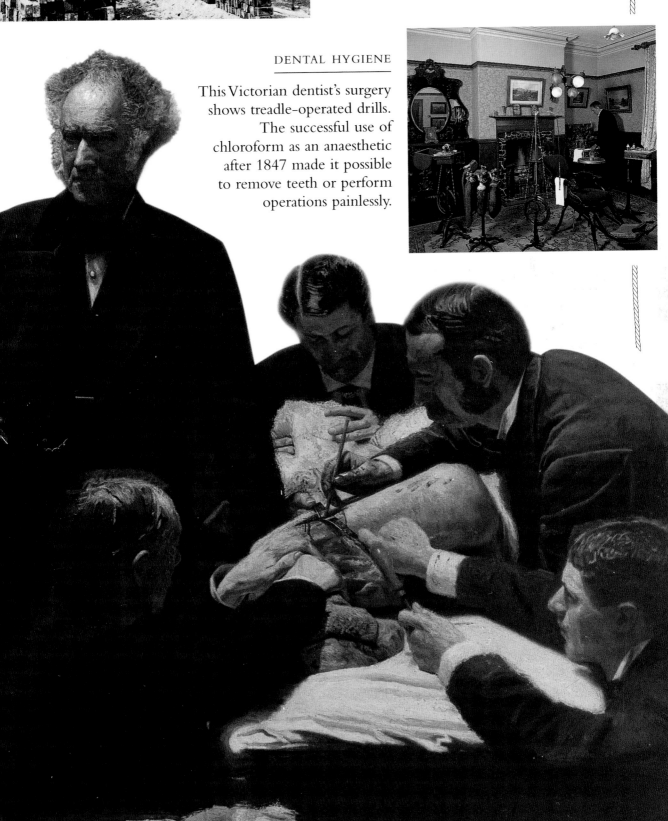

LOVE & MARRIAGE

ARRANGED MARRIAGES

Few marriages were love matches, but were arranged by parents who chose a suitable spouse for their children.

Women from all classes were expected to marry young (usually about age 18) and to raise a family and so were not considered eligible for a career. Upper and middle class girls were usually chaperoned when meeting young men. If a woman had a child out of wedlock she was scorned by society and might become a social outcast, forced to enter a workhouse in order to survive.

OFF TO THE WARS

With so many servicemen deployed around the Empire, many wives were forced to bring up the family single-handed. This picture shows a wife saying farewell to her husband on the eve of his embarkation.

WILD OATS

Young men from wealthy families were often expected to gain sexual experience from liaisons with women of a lower social order, but marriage between people from different classes was frowned upon and might lead to disinheritance from the family estate.

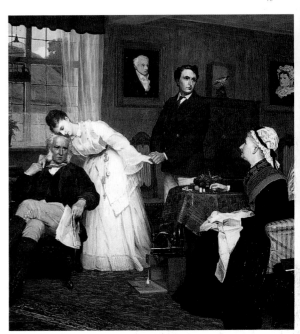

A SPINSTER'S LIFE

Unmarried women were regarded as the property of their fathers, who could also claim any wages they earned. Most parents, however, wanted to see their children married off, particularly daughters, who might have no means of support should anything happen to their fathers.

ROYAL PROPOSAL

According to the dictates of royal protocol, no man is allowed to propose to a queen, so Victoria had to ask for Albert's hand in marriage, unusual for the day. She is seen here surrounded by her children and grandchildren.

WOMEN & CHILDREN

LIFE OF EASE

While boys from wealthy families were groomed for a profession, girls were not expected to work. They spent much of their time entertaining or making social calls to friends and neighbours.

*L*ife for women and children in the 19th century was unbearably hard and few born to poverty had the opportunity to better themselves. Social reformers, like Lord Shaftesbury, did much to improve things and a series of Acts were passed in the 1840s reducing working hours to 10 a day and improving conditions, but unscrupulous employers continued to exploit their workforce.

COMPULSORY EDUCATION

In 1870 the government passed an Education Act stating that all children between the ages of 5-10 must attend school. The education was not free and many poorer families could not afford to send their children. After 1891 schooling became free to all.

VALUABLE 'COMMODITIES'

Women of all classes were regarded as the property of their husbands, as were any wages they earned. Until the Property Act of 1882 all of a woman's property automatically belonged to her husband.

IMPRISONED BY CIRCUMSTANCE

Many women were forced to take their children to prison with them if convicted of a crime, rather than abandon them. Prison reformer Elizabeth Fry helped to improve the often squalid conditions inside and set up schools for the children.

PRISONERS IN THEIR OWN HOMES

The years of innocence in Victorian childhood were short-lived. Children were considered the property of their father, who could send them out to work as young as five years old and keep all their wages to help support the family. Children could be imprisoned in their own homes, a right husbands had even over their wives until 1891.

WOMEN'S EQUALITY?

Women had few rights in 19th century Britain and had to perform the same tasks as men at work, but for much less pay. These ladies were photographed at an iron foundry in South Wales in 1865.

FIRST COLONIES

The British Empire began as a small collection of colonies along the eastern coast of North America. They formed themselves into 13 states, and gained their independence in the reign of Victoria's grandfather, George III. Colonies were also established in what is now Canada during a search for a north-west passage to Asia.

THE MILITARY

Although Britain's Empire was not primarily military led, countries subjected to British rule were held down by a strong military presence.

THE INDIAN MUTI[NY]

Since the 18th century, the East India Company had employed Indian troops. In 1857, these native troops rebelled and a series of bloody battles ensued. The mutiny was eventually crushed and India came under the direct rule of the British Government. In 1876, Victoria became Empress of India, a title all future monarchs retained until India received its independence in 1947.

THE EAST INDIA COMPANY

Elizabethan mariners first landed in India in the 16th century, opening a number of trade routes. In 1600, the East India Company was set up to protect British interests in India and develop further trading contacts with Asia.

28

THE BRITISH EMPIRE . . .

B y the end of Victoria's reign she presided over the largest empire that the world had ever seen. Always conscious of her position as its monarchical head, Victoria was greatly responsible for creating the 'family of nations', later known as the Commonwealth. Unlike other past empires, the interests of the British Empire lay with trade and the wealth it generated, rather than world domination. Although aided by the military, it was not military led, and colonies were acquired in a piecemeal fashion, stretching across the globe.

ORIGINS OF THE EMPIRE

The origins of the British Empire can be traced to the reign of Elizabeth I. In Elizabeth's time, England was often at war with other European nations, particularly Spain who controlled all the major trade routes to the Americas and the East. A series of voyages to uncharted areas of the world became quests for new trade routes and land to establish new colonies.

ROBERT CLIVE

Britain's rule in India began with the victory of Robert Clive in 1757. He defeated the massive combined Indo-French army of 60,000 with a small force of 3,000 men, securing the province of Bengal. Although regarded as a hero back in Britain, Clive was understandably hated by the Indians.

EXTENT OF THE EMPIRE

This map shows the extent of the British Empire (coloured orange) in 1886. All of the major trading routes were under British control, which explains why Britain was such a major influence throughout the world.

BRITISH WAY OF LIFE

When subjugating a new land, the British forced the native people to adopt British ways. Official buildings and houses were built in British styles and British legal and government systems were introduced. The English language became widely-spoken and remains the most dominant language in the world.

EQUAL PORTIONS

Throughout the 18th and 19th centuries there was considerable land-hunger amongst the major world powers. They had the attitude that the world was theirs for the taking and had little regard for the native peoples. This cartoon shows various heads of state dividing up China like a piece of pie, while the Chinese leader looks on helplessly.

THE BRITISH EMPIRE . . .

The British Empire grew slowly. At its fullest extent it covered one quarter of the world's land mass. It reached its zenith immediately after the First World War, when the former German colonies in Africa and Asia were taken over. Because its colonies were scattered across the globe, resources were eventually stretched too thinly. The military were unable to cope and when Britain began to have economic problems at home, the Empire gradually went into decline.

FLYING THE FLAG

The raising of the Union Jack to denote British sovereignty over a newly acquired country was always treated with a great deal of reverence, accompanied by much pomp and ceremony.

VOYAGES OF DISCOVERY

In Elizabethan times, the motives for exploration were quite simple: gold and new trade routes. By Victoria's reign, it was commonplace for explorers to take scientists with them on their voyages, to record and bring back samples of new plants and animal species for scientific study. This practice was started by explorers such as James Cook who is seen here raising the Union Jack in New South Wales, Australia, in 1770.

"NEW CROWNS FOR OLD ONES!"

EMPRESS OF INDIA

In 1876 Queen Victoria was proclaimed Empress of India and was proud to accept the title. She is seen here, in this contemporary cartoon, being asked by Prime Minister Disraeli to trade the imperial crown of India for her own.

THE BRITISH EMPIRE

The reign of Victoria was a golden era, a time when even the Queen herself believed that the 'sun would never set on the Empire'. It coincided with a period of great social and economic change, when Britain led the world in science and technology. Although the British government exploited the colonies, many of them benefited from Britain's developments. Many of the world's railway systems, for example, were built by British engineers, and commodities made in Britain were exported all over the globe. In short, Britain took the world by storm.

FRESH START

One of the strengths of the British Empire lay in colonizing subjugated nations with British citizens. Like these emigrants bound for Sydney, many were keen to try a fresh start in the colonies, faced with poverty and unemployment at home.

THE GERMAN THREAT

The main threat to the Empire came, not from rebelling colonies, but from Germany; more specifically from Victoria's own grandson, Kaiser Wilhelm II. Although Britain's navy was by far the greatest in the world, Germany was able to build warships of the very latest design at a faster rate than Britain could replace its obsolete ones.

BRITANNIA RULES THE WAVES

Four days after Victoria's Diamond Jubilee, in 1897, the Royal Navy staged a massive display of its power at Spithead, on the south coast. It was the largest collection of warships ever assembled and demonstrated to the world the might of the British Empire.

SLAVERY ABOLISHED

Slavery was abolished throughout the Empire in 1833, some years before Victoria's reign. The treatment of native peoples from the colonies was a matter close to the Queen's heart. She strongly resisted giving the Boers of South Africa their independence, for example, fearing they would treat the natives too harshly.

Le Petit Journal
SUPPLÉMENT ILLUSTRÉ

ÉVÉNEMENTS DU TRANSVAAL
Sommation aux Anglais

BRITAIN AT WAR

Throughout Victoria's reign, as Britain greatly extended its empire, there were a number of imperial conflicts. With rising unemployment at home, there was no shortage of manpower to join the ranks of the army. Like Britain, all the other major powers in Europe were keen to acquire new colonies. This jostling for supremacy and land was the cause of one of the worst conflicts in history: the First World War.

BADEN-POWELL

The flamboyant Lieutenant-Colonel, Robert Baden-Powell, became a national hero during the Boer War. He made the small South African trading post of Mafeking his military headquarters and held the town, against 8,000 Boers, with just 1,000 soldiers, losing only 35 men. Baden-Powell went on to form the Boy Scout movement in 1908.

THE BOER WAR
(1899–1902)

The Boers were South African farmers (descended from Dutch settlers) who fiercely resisted Britain's attempts to annexe South Africa after the discovery of gold there. They used guerrilla tactics to combat the massive British force sent against them, but eventually the sheer size of the British army crushed their resistance.

THE CRIMEAN WAR (1854–56)

The Crimean War was fought between Britain and Russia on a peninsula that is now part of modern-day Turkey. Britain was unprepared for the scale of the conflict and suffered one of its worst military disasters, the 'Charge of the Light Brigade', at Balaclava in 1854.

W. NORMAN, (PRIVATE) BRINGING IN SINGLE-HANDED TWO RUSSIAN PRISONERS.

MAB BEACH (PRIVATE) AT INKERMAN, RESCUING COLONEL CARPENTER.

ELTON (MAJOR) WORKING IN THE TRENCHES UNDER A HEAVY FIRE.

FLORENCE NIGHTINGALE

Florence Nightingale (the 'Lady of the Lamp') is best remembered for her work in the Crimean War, tending to the injuries of wounded soldiers. Her reports of the horrors of the Crimea sent shock waves that were felt throughout society. Afterwards, she devoted her life to the better training of nurses.

THE VICTORIA CROSS

During the Crimean War, Victoria had a special medal struck for those who had served in the war. She insisted that no distinction be made between officers and privates – a revolutionary step for the day. She later created the Victoria Cross which is still the highest military honour accorded today.

CRIME & PUNISHMENT

STREET CRIME

Gangs of thieves roamed the dingy streets of Victorian towns at night and often garroted their victims.

*W*ith so much poverty and such appalling living conditions, many people turned to crime as a way of life. Punishments were severe, even for children, who might be imprisoned for stealing a loaf of bread. Prisons were so overcrowded that 'hulks' were moored in river estuaries to house the overspill. Many convicts were sent to the colonies to serve out their sentences.

INDECENT ASSAULT

Victorians were sensitive to moral standards; this music hall dancer was imprisoned for three months on the grounds of indecency for wearing this costume in public.

ROYAL SCAPEGOAT

Many people blamed Victoria herself for their hardships and several attempts were made on her life. This attempt was by an out-of-work Irishman in 1849.

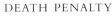

DEATH PENALTY

At the beginning of the 19th century over 200 crimes were punishable by death. Despite reforms, there were still over 70 crimes carrying the death sentence in Victorian times, including petty theft and assault.

WHEEL OF MISFORTUNE

Conditions inside Victorian prisons were cramped and primitive. Treadmills, similar to the one shown here, were used as a form of exercise or to punish unruly prisoners.

A POLICEMAN'S LOT

Until the reform bills of Sir Robert Peel in the 1820s, when a proper civilian police force was set up in London, many criminals got away unpunished. By early Victorian times most towns had their own police force to apprehend villains, often recruited from the armed services and run along similar lines.

TRANSPORT & SCIENCE

SMILE!

Cameras, first developed in the 19th century, were for the first time in history able to record events as they happened, though initially they were used as reconnaissance aids by the military.

Britain's scientists and engineers led the world with their array of technological inventions, such as the development of steam and internal combustion engines, electricity and building techniques. Many of the familiar household objects today, such as light bulbs, typewriters, packaged food and hi-fi had their origins in the Victorian age. Britain became known as the 'workshop of the world'.

IMPROVED ROADS

The first motor cars (invented c.1865) resembled horseless carriages and were open to the elements. They needed metalled surfaces to run effectively, which led to road improvements with the development of tarmacadamed surfaces.

UNDERWATER TACTICS

The development of the submarine and self-propelled torpedoes in both Britain and France changed the face of modern warfare. The one shown here, invented by the Rev. G.W. Garret in 1880 was launched on rails.

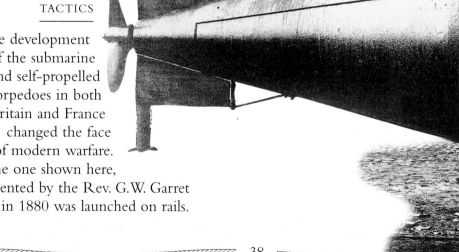

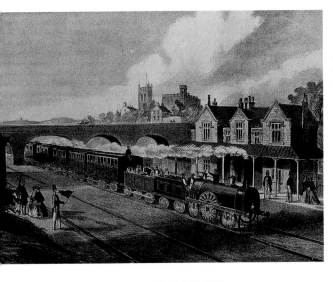

ON THE RIGHT TRACK

The Victorian age saw the rapid development of railways. For the first time in history fast, cheap transport was available to the masses, giving greater mobility to the population. Between 1829 and 1900, 22,000 miles of track were laid in Britain and in 1863 the world's first underground railway was opened in London.

MASS-PRODUCTION

Advancements in technology made it possible to mass-produce economically all manner of items for everyday use that previously had to be individually hand-made at great expense, such as this practical tape measure.

IT'S GOOD TO TALK

The telephone was invented by Alexander Graham Bell in 1875. Although greeted with enthusiasm, it was very expensive to install and initially only available to the rich. It was not possible to dial to another user directly. Connection had to be through an operator. Businessmen, who could better afford them, saw the potential of telephones and benefited enormously from improved communication links.

THE GREAT EXHIBITION

JOSEPH PAXTON

The Crystal Palace building was designed by Joseph Paxton, a brilliant engineer who had erected huge conservatories at stately homes, but this was his masterpiece. It was truly a wonder of the age and prompted Queen Victoria to call it a 'fairy-tale palace'. Paxton received the fee of £5,000 (which is the equivalent of £1 million today) for designing and building it.

The Great Exhibition of 1851 was the brainchild of Prince Albert. He believed that an international exhibition in London would both act as a shop window for British industry and generate more work to benefit the poor. His ideas were not met with enthusiasm by the government but, undaunted, he won popular support and private finance through the press. The exhibition was opened on 1 May 1851 by Queen Victoria and was a resounding success. From then, until its closure on 15 October, over six million people visited the exhibition at a time when Britain's population was only about 20 million. It was the first international trade exhibition in the world.

PREFABRICATED BUILDING

The Crystal Palace, shown here during its original construction, was made of prefabricated parts which enabled the building to be taken down after the exhibition closed in Hyde Park and re-erected some miles away at Sydenham in 1854. The area is still known as Crystal Palace. Sadly, the building burned down in a disastrous fire in 1936.

FROM FAR AND WIDE

Inside the exhibition building there were over 14,000 different exhibitors, over half of whom were from the British Empire. Industrialists from across the globe came to view the best of British industry and place orders for all manner of commodities, from steam trains to spinning machines, textiles to fine art. Admission charges were reduced after two days to ensure that people of all classes could attend.

MUSEUMS FOR ALL

Albert determined that the ordinary people of Britain should benefit from the exhibition; money raised from the proceeds was used to open several large museums in London. These included the Victoria and Albert, the Science and the Natural History Museums, which collectively became the envy of the world.

THE CRYSTAL PALACE

The original exhibition building, erected at Hyde Park, was a masterpiece of cast iron and glass, earning it the title 'The Crystal Palace'. It covered an area of 26 acres and was three times the size of St. Paul's Cathedral. It was about 550 metres (600 yards) long and contained over 300,000 individual panes of glass.

ARRIVING AT THE CAPE

Cape Colony had originally been colonized by the Boers like the ones shown in this picture. When Livingstone arrived in March 1841 it was under British control. He moved north and started his missionary work. By 1849 the urge to travel was too strong and Livingstone joined an expedition to cross the Kalahari Desert. They became the first Europeans to reach Lake Ngami in modern-day Angola.

WORKING AT THE MILL

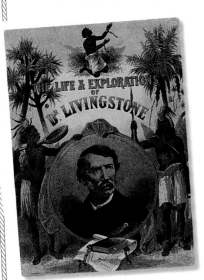

Livingstone started work at a cotton mill next to his house when he was ten years old. He read constantly and soon decided to become a doctor. In 1836 he managed to get to medical school in Glasgow. While he was there he became interested in the work of the London Missionary Society and he decided to do missionary work in China. The Society accepted Livingstone but sent him to southern Africa instead.

GROWING UP IN GLASGOW

David Livingstone was born in 1813 and was brought up on the edge of Glasgow. He shared a single room with his parents, two brothers and two sisters. The room was about four and a half metres square. Although this seems small now, at the time it was regarded as being quite comfortable.

FROM SOLDIER TO JOURNALIST

In 1862 Henry Stanley joined the army. He fought in the American Civil War for the Confederates, who were later to lose the war. Stanley was wounded in his first battle and taken prisoner. After he recovered he became a sailor and later a journalist. He worked for the New York Herald in Europe and Africa, and in 1871 he was sent to find Livingstone.

GREAT EXPLORERS

There have been many great pairs of explorers. Probably the most famous however must be David Livingstone and Henry Stanley, despite the fact that they met only once and spent just a few months together. Between them they opened up more of Africa to the outside world than anybody else, but their reasons for being in Africa could not have been more different. Livingstone was there to spread the Christian gospel and to help put an end to slavery. Stanley came as a journalist seeking the greatest story of his career.

WHO WAS HENRY STANLEY?

Henry Stanley's real name was John Rowlands. He was born in Wales in 1841, the year that Livingstone arrived in Africa. He lived with his father and then moved into a workhouse where he received a basic education. When he was 15 he sailed from Liverpool to New Orleans where he started work in a shop owned by a man called Henry Stanley.

LIVINGSTONE'S FAMILY JOINS AN EXPEDITION

This picture shows Livingstone on another expedition in 1851 to explore the rivers around Lake Ngami. He took with him his pregnant wife and their three children. In August he arrived at the mighty Zambezi River. He decided to explore it further, and when his family returned to Britain in June 1852 he returned on his greatest expedition yet.

GREAT EXPLORERS

THE DEATH OF LIVINGSTONE

When Stanley left Livingstone in March 1872 he left behind a sick and weak man. But Livingstone did not die until 1 May 1873. His African companions, including his servant Chuma pictured here, preserved his body and carried it over 2,000 kilometres to the coast. Livingstone was buried at Westminster Abbey and mourned as a national hero.

When Livingstone set off on his second expedition in June 1852, he explored more of the Zambezi River and was the first white person to see the Victoria Falls. He went on two more expeditions in 1858 and 1866. Livingstone was away for so long on the last expedition that most people in Britain assumed that he was dead. The New York Herald sent Stanley to discover if this wa true. After five months Stanley returned to Europe to tel an expectant public of his adventures. Livingstone remained in Africa and died there in May 1873.

VICTORIA FALLS

For three years from 1852 to 1855 Livingstone had been following the Zambezi River downstream. Frequent illness and low supplies often slowed the expedition down. However, on 16 November 1855 Livingstone saw the Victoria Falls. The local name for the Falls was 'Mosi-oa-Tunya' which meant 'smoke that thunders'. Livingstone decided to rename it after the British queen.

FIGHTING THE SLAVE TRADE

Livingstone was determined to fight the slave trade, a feeling strengthened in July 1871 when he witnessed a massacre of over 400 Africans by Arab slavers. Stanley brought back news of this massacre and the strength of public opinion forced the British government to take action against the slavers. Ironically, Stanley became notorious for treating his African porters harshly.

STANLEY AND LIVINGSTONE MEET

Led by an African carrying the American flag Stanley travelled over 800 kilometres inland from the East African coast. As Stanley approached Ujiji on the shores of Lake Tanganyika he was told that a white man was staying there. Stanley walked into Ujiji. He stepped up to Livingstone and said *'Doctor Livingstone, I Presume?'*

RELIGION

To most Christians, up to Victorian times, the Bible was taken as literal truth and few people questioned its authenticity. When Charles Darwin and others challenged this view with their revolutionary theories of evolution by natural selection, they shattered the beliefs of ordinary people and clergy alike. Many were unable to reconcile their religious feelings with the new scientific theories and Darwin suffered open derision from the public throughout his life.

CHALLENGE TO THE CHURCH

The biologist Thomas Huxley championed Darwin's theories of evolution when the church attacked his views and tried to discredit him as a heretic.

SUNDAY SCHOOLS

For many working class children, who worked all week, Sunday or charity schools, organised by the church, were the only form of education they received. Apart from learning to read, the only other subject usually taught was Bible studies.

A religious fervour and strict moral upbringing swept Victorian society, particularly the upper and middle classes. For the first time since the Reformation many new churches were built, or medieval ones restored. At the beginning of Victoria's reign (1837) about 60% of the population regularly went to church on Sundays; today the figure is less than 1%.

THE DESCENT OF MAN

When Charles Darwin published 'The Origin of the Species' in 1859 he caused a furore by challenging the biblical account of the Creation, in which God created man in his own likeness. According to Darwin, man evolved gradually from an ape-like creature over many thousands of years.

THE 'SALLY ARMY'

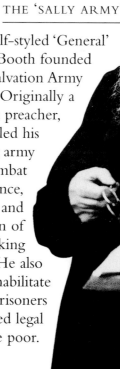

The self-styled 'General' William Booth founded the Salvation Army in 1878. Originally a Methodist preacher, he modelled his church along army lines to combat intemperance, prostitution and exploitation of the working classes. He also helped rehabilitate discharged prisoners and introduced legal aid for the poor.

THE OXFORD MOVEMENT

Evangelicalism had its origins in Oxford. A group of like-minded men felt that the Anglican Church had become lax in its duties towards the poor and so formed a new church with a more humanitarian doctrine.

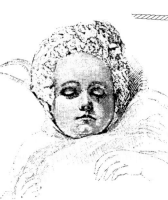

THE YOUNG VICTORIA

Victoria was born at Kensington Palace and was christened exactly one month later in the Cupola Room at the Palace. There was a dispute over her name, her parents eventually settling on Alexandrina Victoria as her registered name, but they called her Victoria from birth.

*W*hen Victoria was born on 24 Ma 1819 she was fifth in line to the throne and the likelihood of her succeeding seemed very remote. Her grandfather, George III, was still king and ahead of her in succession were her uncles, George, the Prince Regent, the Dukes of York and Clarence, and of course her father, the Duke of Kent. Within a short space of time, however, all that changed. Her father died unexpectedly on 23 January 1820 followed, six days later, by her grandfather.

The Duke of York died in 1827, taking her a step nearer the throne. Her remaining uncles succeeded as George IV and William IV, respectively, but their failing health produced no heirs, leaving Victoria as heir to the throne.

PERSONAL POSSESSIONS

Many of Queen Victoria's personal possessions still survive, a number of them on view at the Victoria and Albert Museum. These reading glasses once belonged to the Queen; the case is inscribed with her personal insignia.

WILLIAM IV

Victoria's uncle, William IV, became King at the age of 64 on the death of his brother, and when he died in 1837 he left no legitimate heirs to the throne. Victoria became queen as his closest living relative.

THE YOUNG PRINCESS

Always a friendly and playful child (who had no fewer than 132 dolls!), she had an aptitude for music, singing and dancing and was an accomplished artist. She spoke with a strong German accent as a child, because of her mother's German origins, and she could speak German and French fluently.

THE QUEEN COMES OF AGE

Princess Victoria was just 18 years old when she heard of the death of her uncle, William IV, in 1837. She was immediately filled with feelings of both happiness and sadness, but seems to have assumed the awesome responsibility with apparent calm. She was crowned the following year, on 28 June, at Westminster Abbey. Not a popular figure at first, she was destined to become Britain's longest reigning monarch and ruler over the greatest empire the world has ever seen.

DUCHESS OF KENT

Victoria's father was Edward, Duke of Kent, fourth son of George III. Victoria never knew her father, who died when she was a baby. Her mother, the Duchess of Kent, was appointed Regent in case Victoria succeeded to the throne whilst still a child.

PRINCE ALBERT

One of the first dilemmas facing Victoria when she succeeded to the throne was that of marriage. Lord Melbourne, the Prime Minister, advised Victoria to marry as soon as possible to create her own heirs. At first she had no interest in doing so but agreed to meet her cousin, Prince Albert of Saxe-Coburg-Gotha. Both entered the relationship reluctantly at first, but there seems to have been a mutual attraction and they soon became very dear friends.

After marriage their friendship developed into a very deep and genuine love for one another and they became a devoted couple.

THE PRINCE CONCORT

Prince Albert was, in Victoria's own words, '*so sensible, so kind, and so good, and so amiable...the most pleasing and delightful exterior and appearance you can possibly see.*' He was tall, intelligent and proved to be a very able political adviser to Victoria. He took a genuine interest in his new adoptive country, particularly the poorer classes. He is credited with re-introducing the practice of bringing decorated Christmas trees into the house, a custom still practised in his native Germany, though it had long fallen out of favour in England.

THE ROYAL WEDDING

The wedding between Victoria and Albert took place on 10 February 1840 at St. James's Palace. They were both just 20 years old. She wore a white satin gown with a lace flounce, and a Turkish diamond necklace and sapphire brooch (a present from Albert). The couple were well received by the public. After the wedding reception held at Buckingham Palace, they had a three-day honeymoon at Windsor Castle.

THE PRINCE DIES

In 1861 Prince Albert contracted typhoid and died prematurely, at the age of 42. The Queen was heartbroken. The prospect of facing the world alone culminated in a nervous breakdown. She wore black for the rest of her life in respect for Albert. t first the public sympathized with er, but after over a decade of ourning, there were calls for er abdication.

THE QUEEN PROPOSES

According to the dictates of royal protocol, no man is allowed to propose to a queen, so Victoria had to ask for Albert's hand in marriage. She proposed to him on 15 October 1839. In her diary, Victoria wrote that Albert's acceptance was the brightest and happiest moment of her life.

KEEPSAKES

To commemorate the royal wedding a great many mementoes were made, such as this decorative lustre-ware jug.

EVENTS OF VICTORIA'S LIFE

~1819~
Victoria born at Kensington Palace

~1820~
Victoria's father Edward, Duke of Kent, dies

~1830~
George IV dies; William IV accedes to the throne

~1833~
Slavery abolished throughout the Empire

~1834~
Poor Law creates workhouses for the poor

Houses of Parliament burn down

~1837~
William IV dies; Victoria accedes to the throne

~1838~
Victoria's coronation

People's Charter issued, calling for political reform

~1840~
Victoria marries Albert of Saxe-Coburg-Gotha

~1840~
Princess 'Vicky' born (Victoria's first child)

~1845~
Beginning of Irish potato famine

~1846~
Corn Laws repealed

FAMILY LIFE

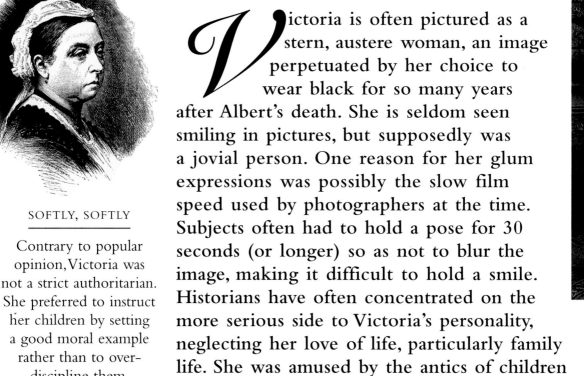

*V*ictoria is often pictured as a stern, austere woman, an image perpetuated by her choice to wear black for so many years after Albert's death. She is seldom seen smiling in pictures, but supposedly was a jovial person. One reason for her glum expressions was possibly the slow film speed used by photographers at the time. Subjects often had to hold a pose for 30 seconds (or longer) so as not to blur the image, making it difficult to hold a smile. Historians have often concentrated on the more serious side to Victoria's personality, neglecting her love of life, particularly family life. She was amused by the antics of children and both she and Albert enjoyed simple, family pastimes. In later life, Victoria loved to see herself as the great matriarch.

SOFTLY, SOFTLY

Contrary to popular opinion, Victoria was not a strict authoritarian. She preferred to instruct her children by setting a good moral example rather than to over-discipline them.

THE GRANDMOTHER OF EUROPE

This picture, taken in 1897, shows the extended family of Queen Victoria. The Prince of Wales (and future king Edward VII) stands immediately to her left. By the various marriages of her children and grand-children, Victoria was related to all of the major royal houses of Europe, including Germany, Norway, Sweden, Greece, Spain, Romania and Russia, earning her the affectionate title 'the grandmother of Europe'.

HAPPY FAMILIES

In keeping with most families of the day, Victoria and Albert had many children, nine in all. She gave birth to Princess Victoria (Vicky) in November 1840. Vicky, the Princess Royal, remained a close friend throughout the Queen's life, especially after Albert's death. Victoria's family life was, by all accounts, a happy one. It is difficult to say what kind of relationship she had with all her children: some accounts claim she was aloof and dispassionate, others paint a rosier picture. There does appear to have been real animosity between her and Edward, the future king, whom she thought foolish, and was critical of his behaviour.

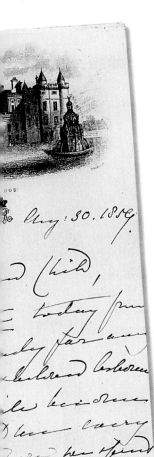

Aug: 30. 1819.

PERSONAL RECOLLECTIONS

We know a great deal about the personal life and opinions of Queen Victoria from her diary, which she maintained throughout her life. It was not, as many suppose, a secret diary, certainly not in her younger years, because it was frequently perused by her mother and governess.

EVENTS OF VICTORIA'S LIFE

~1853~
Vaccination against smallpox made compulsory

~1854~
Crimean War breaks out between Britain (and France) and Russia

~1856~
Victoria Cross first introduced for bravery in wartime

~1857~
Indian Mutiny against British rule

~1861~
Prince Albert dies; Victoria goes into mourning and withdraws from public life

~1867~
Canada becomes first country within British Empire to be declared an independent dominion

New Houses of Parliament opened

~1870~
Primary Education made compulsory for all children

~1871~
Trade Unions legalized

~1874~
Victoria comes out of mourning and resumes her public duties

ASSASSINATION ATTEMPTS

At the beginning of her reign Victoria was not a popular figure at all. As ruling monarch, she was often seen as the cause of social discontent; some would have preferred a king on the throne. There were several attempts made on Victoria's life including this attempt in 1840 by Edward Oxford.

REFORM ACTS

During her reign, Victoria approved several Act of Parliament that had important social and constitutional implications. Growing unrest in Britain meant new political movements were forcing change. In 1838 the Chartists issued th 'Peoples' Charter' which called for political reform. Although not fully realized until 1944, it forms the basis of our parliamentary system today. In 1867 and 1884, the Second and Third Reform Acts extended the right to vote to more people.

FATHER FIGURE

During the early years of her reign Victoria relied heavily on the advice of Lord Melbourne, the Whig (Liberal) Prime Minister, who guided her through the intricacies of politics and her role in government.

SOCIAL CHANGE

The Industrial Revolution saw Britain change from a mainly agricultural nation to an industrial one. People who left the country to seek employment in the towns were exploited by greedy industrialists. Trade unionists like Joseph Arch founder of the Nationa Union of Farm Labourer (shown right), fought long and hard battle fo workers' rights. Trad unions were finall legalized in 1871

VICTORIA & GOVERNMENT

From the beginning Victoria showed a genuine interest in the government of the country and developed a good rapport with most of the leading politicians of the day. She took her role seriously and, whilst accepting the relatively new idea of a constitutional monarchy (which meant that she had no real part to play in politics), she also realized that she had considerable influence and exercised her powers wisely. Albert, who had shown little interest in politics prior to their marriage, also took an active role in matters of government.

POLITICAL GIANTS

Victoria witnessed the coming and going of several great politicians, including William Gladstone and Benjamin Disraeli. Victoria liked Disraeli (above) and had him invested Earl of Beaconsfield, whereas Gladstone frequently incurred her wrath.

A NEW HOUSE FOR PARLIAMENT

Until the reign of Victoria's uncle, William IV, Parliament met in the old royal palace of Westminster. Like most medieval buildings, it contained a lot of wood and burned down in a disastrous fire in 1834. The present Houses of Parliament were rebuilt on part of the old palace site. Victoria officiated at the opening of the new building in 1867.

THE ROYAL PALACES

BUCKINGHAM PALACE

The population census of 1841 shows Buckingham Palace to be Queen Victoria's main residence. It is still the residence most often associated with British royalty but is a relative newcomer to the list of royal palaces. Victoria's grandfather, George III, purchased the house for £28,000 in 1762. The state apartments are magnificent, and frequently host state functions.

*V*ictoria and Albert made full use of the royal palaces. For official duties, balls and government functions they favoured Buckingham Palace (shown here in 1852), but the Queen always preferred the privacy of Windsor Castle. As a young girl Victoria enjoyed the hurly-burly of London's social scene, but Albert was a country man at heart, preferring the peace and solitude of the country estates. Later in life, Victoria also came to prefer them.

OSBORNE HOUSE

In 1844, Victoria and Albert began looking for a house to which they could retire from the hustle and bustle of court life. The Osborne estate on the Isle of Wight proved ideal, and Prince Albert designed and built a new house in Italian Renaissance style.

BALMORAL CASTLE

This view shows part of Victoria's private apartments (the drawing room) at Balmoral Castle in Aberdeenshire. Surrounded by mountains and set in 30,000 acres of deer forest, Balmoral has always been a royal favourite since it was purchased and redesigned by Prince Albert in 1853.

WINDOR CASTLE

Windsor Castle is the oldest royal residence in Britain and also the largest inhabited castle in the world. Begun by William the Conqueror in 1066 it has been greatly extended since then. Successive monarchs, right up to George IV, Victoria's uncle, continued the process of transforming the great medieval castle into a magnificent palace.

THE JUBILEE YEARS

MEMENTOES OF
A SPECIAL DAY

For Victoria's Golden and Diamond Jubilees, many people were given the day off work and most remembered the day by buying specially-made souvenirs.

*T*he last years of Victoria's reign were a marked contrast to the early years. Although she eventually came out of mourning for Albert some 13 years after his death (in 1874), she never got over his loss She returned to public life, but with advancing years the queen became a sadder, more melancholic person. Victoria had not been universally popular throughout her reign. Many had not welcomed her to the throne, but by the time of her Golden Jubilee in 1887 she was at the height of her popularity.

NEVER-TO-BE-FORGOTTEN-DAY

The Queen's Golden Jubilee marked 50 years of her reign. People throughout the Empire celebrated the event, particularly in Britain itself (and more especially in London) with wild enthusiasm. Victoria said of the occasion: '*This never-to-be-forgotten day will always leave the most gratifying and heart-stirring memories behind.*'

FAMILY GATHERING

On the occasion of her Golden Jubilee, Victoria attended a banquet held in her honour in Buckingham Palace. Invited guests included all the crowned heads of Europe, most of whom were related to Victoria. For her Diamond Jubilee in 1897, as this portrait shows, the gathering was of her 'extended family' and colonial premiers from countries throughout the Empire.

THE DIAMOND JUBILEE

This painting shows Queen Victoria arriving at St. Paul's Cathedral for a thanksgiving service on 22 June 1897, held in honour of her Diamond Jubilee. Out of respect for her age and ailing health the service was kept deliberately short.

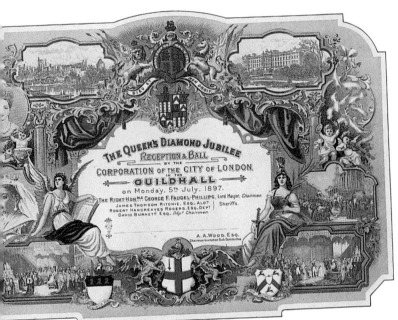

ROYAL INVITE

This picture shows one of the formal invitations to the Queen's Diamond Jubilee celebrations at the Guildhall in London, one of many public functions held throughout the country. By this time the Queen was a frail old lady with bad rheumatism and failing eyesight, confined to a wheelchair. However, she continued to perform her duties right up until a few weeks before she died.

THE END OF AN ERA

FAMILY FEUDS

This family tree shows that most of Victoria's children married into the royal houses of Europe, which she hoped would have a stabilizing effect on European politics. Sadly, this was not to be.

With the death of Victoria on 22 January 1901, it really was the end of an era. In some respects Victoria was liberal in her attitude, taking a keen interest in improving the living conditions of the poor, but in other ways she was very conservative. She frowned upon the idea of women holding professions, yet she objected strongly to the working conditions imposed on women and children in the mines and factories. Similarly, she opposed giving the vote to women, but supported giving the vote to working class men. Britain had seen more change during her reign than in any other period in history, but the world was now poised on the threshold of a whole new age.

THREAT TO PEACE

This picture shows the Kaiser, William II, Victoria's grandson by the marriage of her daughter Vicky to Prince Frederick of Prussia. Victoria always resented his anti-British views, but he was at her bedside when she lay dying. Had she lived a few more years she would have seen him lead Germany against Britain in the First World War.

PROBLEM CHILD

This view shows Victoria with her son, the future King Edward VII, shortly before her death. She was always critical of Edward and did not feel he had the necessary qualities to make a good king. She deliberately kept him out of government issues for fear his head-strong attitude might create problems. In later life she finally acknowledged him as her heir.

TRUSTED ADVISER

Victoria followed a high moral code in life, but she was no stranger to scandal. During her period of mourning for Albert she befriended a Scots servant called John Brown, an excellent horseman, who the Queen trusted and took into her confidence. He became her constant companion and rumours began to circulate they were having an affair, causing her popularity to sink to an all-time low.

EVENTS OF VICTORIA'S LIFE

~1876~
Victoria becomes 'Empress' of India

~1887~
Independent Labour Party founded

~1897~
Victoria's Diamond Jubilee celebrates 60 years on the throne

~1899~
Boer War breaks out in South Africa

~1901~
Queen Victoria dies; our longest reigning monarch

Edward VII accedes to the throne

FAMILY PORTRAIT

This family portrait was taken at Osborne House in 1898, three years before Victoria's death. When she died, her body was taken from there to Cowes and on to London. Her funeral was carried out according to her own instructions and she was buried at Frogmore, sharing the same mausoleum as her beloved husband, Prince Albert.

INDEX

Picture Credits:
t=top, b=bottom, c=centre, l=left, r=right, OFC=outside front cover, IFC=inside front cover,
IBC=inside back cover, OBC=outside back cover

The Games Room, 1889, Jean Beraud © ADAGP, Paris and DACS, London 1997 (Musee Carnavalet, Paris/Giraudon/Bridgeman Art Library, London); 14b. Ann Ronan at Image Select International Ltd; 28l, 28/29c, 29tr, 31b, 32b, 32tl, 33tl, 33tr, 34bl, 34/35cb, 35cr & 35br, 40tl, 40bl, 48tl, 48br, 50r, 51c, 52bl, 52tl, 54tr, 54c, 55tr, 55bl, 60tl, 61tr. The Bridgeman Art Library, London; 28/29cb, 30t, 31bl, 33bl & 33br, 41tl, 49br, 49tl, 49t, 50l, 51bl, 53tl, 54bl, 56/57 (main image), 57tr, 58bl, 58tl, 59cl, 60/61c. Bridgeman - Giraudon; 59tr.. By courtesy of BT Archives; 39cr. B.T. Batsford Ltd; 8/9b. Barnado's Photographic Archive (D58); 10bl. The Beamish. The North of England Open Air Museum; 21cr. Bodleian Library, University of Oxford; John Johnson Collectionn; Political General folder 1;6l, 7br., Trades and Possessions 8; 6/7b, Educational 16; 11tr, Trade in Prints and Scraps 9; 15cl, Trade in Prints and Scraps 7; 22l. Food 2; 22cb, Alphabets 3; 46-47t. Chris Fairclough Colour Library at Image Select International Ltd; 55br, 57c. Fine Art Photographic Library; 35t. FORBES Magazine Collection, New York/Bridgeman Art Library, London; 8bl, 25cr, 47tr. Christopher Wood Gallery, London/Bridgeman Art Library, London; 11tl; 14/15b. Image Select International Ltd; 30tr, 40/41c, 56tl, 60/61cb, 60bl. Mary Evans Picture Library, London; 30br, 34tl, 41br, 51tl, 56/57c, 59b. Spectrum Colour Library; 31tr. Marylebone Cricket Club, London/Bridgeman Art Library, London; 14l. Jefferson College, Philadelphia/Bridgeman Art Library, London; 19b. The Fotomas Index (London); 29br. 48bl, 52/53cb. Guildhall Art Gallery, Corporation of London/Bridgeman Art Library, London; 24b. Mary Evans Picture Library; 5tl, 5tr, 5c, 7tl, 7tr, 14cr, 15cr, 18tl. By courtesy of Fine Art Photographic Library; 17tr, 18/19b, 19t, 24tl, 39t, 46b. Galerie Berko/Fine Art Photographic Library; 10-11b, 13t. Haynes Fine Art/Fine Art Photographic Library; 8t. Hollywood Road Gallery/Fine Art Photographic Library; 16bl. N.R. Omell Gallery/Fine Art Photographic Library; 9r. Polak Gallery/Fine Art Photographic Library; 15t, 26tl, 26bl. Sutcliffe Galleries/Fine Art Photographic Library; 3br, 23tl. Guildhall Library, Corporation of London; 5c, 10br. From the John Hillelson Collection; 8tl, 37cr. Hulton Getty; 4l 9tl, 16tl, 23tl, 25br, 46tl. Hunting Aerofims Ltd (Mills 147); 15br. The Illustrated London News Picture Library; 37tl. Museum of London; 16/17t, 16/17b, 17br. By courtesy of the National Portrait Gallery, London; 19cr. Oxfordshire Photographic Archive, DLA, OCC; 4r, 12l, 47bl. Popperfoto; 27br. Rural History Centre, University of Reading; 13cb. The Salvation Army International Heritage Centre; 47br. Science Museum /Science & Society Picture Library; 8/9c, 13cl, 22tr, 38tl, 38/39b, 39c.

ACKNOWLEDGEMENTS

We would like to thank: Graham Rich, Tracey Pennington, Liz Rowe and Peter Done for their assistance.
Copyright © 2006 *ticktock* Entertainment Ltd.
First published in Great Britain in 1997 by *ticktock* Publishing Ltd., Unit 2, Orchard Business Centre, North Farm Road,
Tunbridge Wells, Kent TN2 3EH. All rights reserved.
No part of this publication may be reproduced, stored in a retrieval system, or transmitted in any form or by any means electronic, mechanical,
photocopying, recording or otherwise, without prior written permission of the copyright owner.
A CIP catalogue record for this book is available from the British Library. ISBN 1 86007 635 1
Picture research by Image Select. Printed in China.

Every effort has been made to trace the copyright holders and we apologise in advance for any unintentional omissions.
We would be pleased to insert the appropriate acknowledgement in any subsequent edition of this publication.